D0931667

The Godfather

CLASSIC QUOTES

"It's really a novel about family."
— Mario Puzo

"I look at it as the story of a king with three sons."
— Francis Ford Coppola

CONTENTS

A History of THE GODFATHER

AMERIGO BONASERA sat in New York Criminal Court Number 3 and waited for justice; vengeance on the men who had so cruelly hurt his daughter, who had tried to dishonor her..," So begins the novel, *The Godfather*, written by Mario Puzo, that was published by G.P. Putnam's Sons on March 10, 1969.

Puzo was 49 years old at the time of its publication. After years of writing books that were well-received but barely paid the bills, the monetarily challenged Puzo had finally struck gold. By the end of 1969 alone, the book had sold more than 350,000 hardcover copies. By the end of 1971, the novel had sold more than 1,000,000 copies in hardcover and 8,000,000 copies in paperback. It was a *Literary Guild Main Selection*. Bill Targ

Puzo's editor at Putnam, shocked the long-suffering writer when he informed him that the paperback rights to *The Godfather* had been sold to Fawcett for the highest six-figure price in Putnam's history – a then-staggering $410,000! Today, *The Godfather* is generally regarded as one of the best-selling books of the 1970s.

The controversial book garnered the public's attention for its powerful and engrossing story, as well as its violence. *Publisher's Weekly* praised it as a book of "absorbing fiction"that possessed "an engrossing climax." In *Newsweek*, the famous Pete Axthelm called it, "a big, turbulent, highly entertaining novel," labeling Puzo "an extremely talented storyteller" whose novel "moves at breakneck speed without ever losing its balance."

Axthelm went so far as to hail Puzo as a "social historian," and the novel a work of fiction and yet a "valid and fascinating portrait of America's most powerful and least understood subculture, the Mafia."

In his *New York Times Book Review*, Dick Schapp wrote, "Puzo has written a solid story that you can read without discomfort at one long sitting." Gay Talese praised the book in *The Washington Post Book World*, for its "marvelous sections" highlighting Don Corleone's familial relationships and for the "excellent sections on the logistics of the numbers operation, the organizational structure of the underworld, [and] the roles that various people play." Talese commented that tales of the mafia, fiction or non-fiction, are always popular reading. "It works beautifully in real life, as readers of newspapers know, and it works equally beautifully in this book." "The hypothesis that the popularity of the book is due to the ability of readers to identify with and care about the members of the Mafia is clearly only one of many possible explanations for the popularity of the book. One thing which is certain, however, is the lasting impact the book has had on American culture. The book was not only a hit in 1969, but it continues to influence books and movies today," opines Jennifer Crist in her book, 20th-Century American Bestsellers.

When it was time to make the movie version, Francis Ford Coppola was chosen to direct the film. He had directed several minor films previously, with little popular acclaim, though he had won an Academy Award® for co-writing Patton, the movie starring George C. Scott, in 1970. Puzo and Coppola set about writing the screenplay together. The main part of shooting took place between March 29 and August 6 of 1971. A scene featuring Al Pacino and Diane Keaton at Connie Corleone's wedding was shot in autumn of that year.

Coppola was actually the studio's third choice to direct, and tension between him and Paramount Pictures remained high throughout

some cost overruns, Coppola eventually got most of what he wanted, including casting Marlon Brando as Don Vito Corleone and Al Pacino as Michael Corleone. It was so hot a role in Hollywood that Jack Nicholson, Dustin Hoffman, Warren Beatty, Martin Sheen, James Caan and Robert De Niro auditioned for the part of Michael Corleone. Anthony Perkins auditioned for the parts of Sonny Corleone, eventually played by James Caan, as well as Tom Hagen, played by Robert Duvall. Paul Newman and Steve McQueen also auditioned for the part of Tom Hagen.

In the opening scene of the movie, Puzo and Coppola stayed true to the book, giving Bonasera the

America has made my fortune. And I raised my daughter in the American fashion. I gave her freedom, but - I taught her never to dishonor her family." Like the book, the movie was a controversial smash hit.

The Godfather was nominated for 11 Academy Awards® in 1972, and came away with 3 of the best of the Oscars®: Best Picture; Best Screenplay Based on Material from Another Medium (Puzo/Coppola); and Best Actor for Marlon Brando.

THE MAGIC LIVES ON

Today, movie watchers, reviewers, critics, and historians all hail The Godfather as a cinematic masterpiece. It was voted Greatest Film of All Time by Entertainment Weekly [1], and #3 of all time by the Amer-

ican Film Institute. TV Guide's "Movie Guide" said of it, "One of the central American movies of the last 25 years, and one of very few to succeed as both popular entertainment and high art." The Godfather has been placed among such cinematic achievements as Citizen Kane, Gone With the Wind, and other landmark films.

THE GODFATHER CLASSIC QUOTES

"Coppola's masterpiece reveals something new every time you watch it," wrote Neil Smith of the BBC in his review of The Godfather. It continues to be a top earner for video and DVD sales and rentals, and millions have seen the movie worldwide. One of the perennially provocative themes of the movie – and the book – is the wisdom that is passed down by its characters from generation to generation. Like Machiavelli's *The Prince* or Sun Tsu's *Art of War*, Coppola's and Puzo's story has provided an endless amount of advice and insight on strategy and common sense for people the world over. Its most memorable lines are now part of our collective consciousness – lines like, "I'll make him an offer he can't refuse," and, "You spend time with your family? Good. Cause a man who doesn't spend time with his family can never be a real man," and, "This is business, not personal." Then there's "Leave the gun. Take the cannolis."

"Being a professional mobster isn't all sunshine and roses," wrote Roger Ebert in the *Chicago Sun-Times* when he reviewed the movie in January of 1972. "More often, it's the boredom of stuffy rooms and a bad diet of carry-out food, punctuated by brief, terrible bursts of violence. This is exactly the feel of 'The Godfather,' which brushes aside the flashy glamour of the traditional gangster picture and gives us what's left: fierce tribal loyalties, deadly little neighborhood quarrels in Brooklyn, and a form of vengeance to match every affront."

Obviously, the main protagonist is Don Vito Corleone, played "skillfully" by Marlon Brando, according to Ebert. "His voice is wheezy and whispery, and his physical movements deliberately lack precision; the effect is of a man so accustomed to power that he no longer needs to remind others."

But the wisdom is sometimes in the unlikeliest of places, whether it comes from Pete Clemenza, the fat *caporegime*, would-be drug czar Virgil Solozzo, Michael Corleone - or others - the movie and story are consummate studies of power and how to wield it - lightly, moderately, or with utter brutality - and when to use which. Each person who wields power does so differently. Don Vito and Michael are thoughtful, Sonny is hot headed, Solozzo is sneaky, and Don Barzini the most Machiavellian. It is a giant, violent, and bloody chess match played out on the chessboard that is the streets of New York.

"*The Godfather*' is a handbook on cinematic lucidity. All events are described clearly. Motives of all the characters are set right there on the table next to the pasta for our consideration," wrote Barbara Schulgasser for the *San Francisco Examiner*." From the opening moments, we understand the authority that rests in Don Corleone (Marlon Brando). That he is a powerful man is as explicit as the fact that he wields that power mercifully, within the context of the murder and mayhem that naturally goes with his territory. The Don is the head of a renegade organization, and, yes, he's a criminal with politicians in his pocket. But he has integrity. "

As Ebert wrote, "We tend to identify with Don Corleone's family not because we dig gang wars, but because we have been with them from the beginning, watching them wait for battle while sitting at the kitchen table and eating chow mein out of paper cartons." No one is saying crime lords or mobsters are good men, but like generals and presidents, they must consider each action and how it will affect, first, their family and their enterprises, as well as the lives of people under their command and protection - to how their actions will reverberate in the world in which they live. It is a fact that many modern mobsters, both American and international, have taken their cues on how to act and interact from this powerful movie series. What an interesting twist of fate.

The references to the power of the story have also woven their way into American politics, with the great writer Russell Baker scribbling, "A group of politicians deciding to dump a President because his morals are bad is like the Mafia getting together to bump off the Godfather for not going to church on Sunday."

And even legendary mobsters like Sammy "the Bull" Gravano, caporegime under real-life Don John Gotti, said, "I loved *The Godfather*. I thought that was the best interpretation of our life that I've ever seen." Brando himself once joked, "I'd gotten to know quite a few *mafiosi*, and all of them told me they loved the picture because I had played the Godfather with dignity. Even today I can't pay a check in Little Italy."

"All the wiseguys I've spoken to love *"The Godfather"* because it makes them out to be men of honor, men who kill only when they need to or take only the things that are rightfully theirs.

The films made gangsters look much more glamorous and benevolent than they really are. Yes, they have a code, lots of rules, but they break those rules all the time," says veteran crime journalist and best-selling author Jerry Capeci.

Another highly acclaimed crime reporter, George Anastaia, says, "*Godfather I* and *II* are classic movies. They get into the fantasy and myth of the mob. At some point there must have been some nobility and some honor."

No matter which side of the equation you consider - good or bad - the Corleone family and their attendant cadre of soldiers and adversaries inhabit a fascinating world. They each have a part to

understand the universal themes that motivate and inspire us in our daily lives: love, family, power, business, reason, success, ambition, and so many more. Find yours in these words of wisdom from *The Godfather*.

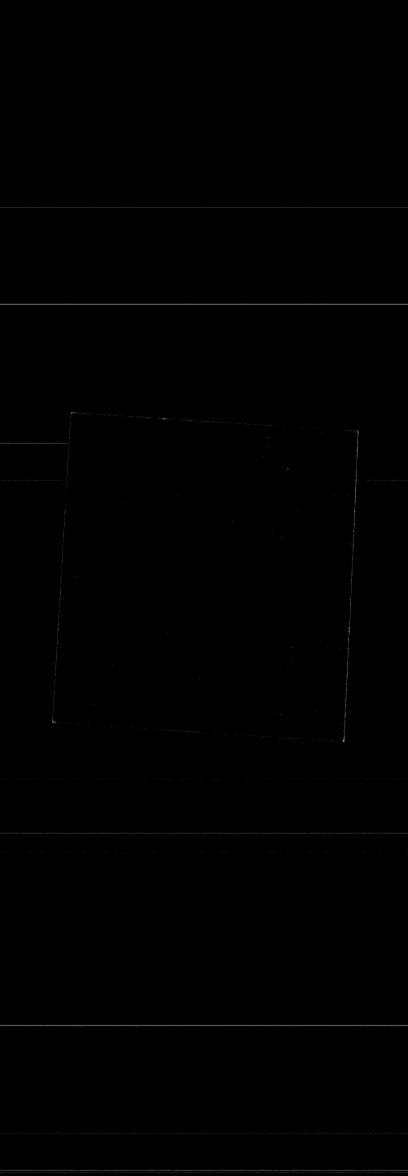

The Godfather

CLASSIC QUOTES

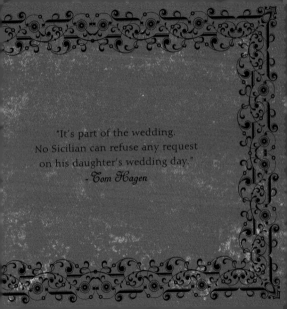

"It's part of the wedding.
No Sicilian can refuse any request
on his daughter's wedding day."
- Tom Hagen

"Luca Brasi held a gun to his head -
and my father assured him that
either his brains or his signature
would be on the contract."
- *Michael Corleone*

Mr & Mrs. Vito Corleone

**REQUEST THE HONOR OF YOUR PRESENCE
AT THE WEDDING OF THEIR DAUGHTER**

Miss Constanzia Francesca Corleone

TO

Mister Carlo Pietro Rizzi

ON AUGUST 25, 1945 · At Noon

**Our Lady Queen of Martyr's Church
110-06 Queens Blvd.
Forest Hills, NY 11375**

RECEPTION TO FOLLOW

"You spent time with your family?
Good. Because a man who doesn't spend
time with his family can never be a real man."
- *Don Vito Corleone*

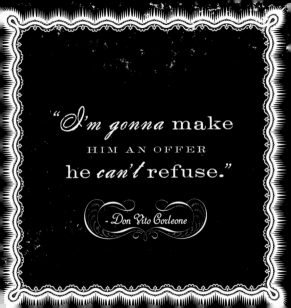

"Give him

but

Fami

a *living*

never discuss the

y business

with him."

- Don Vito Corleone

"There you are — six-hundred thousand dollars
on four hooves. I'll bet Russian czars
never paid that kinda dough for a single horse.
Karthom. Karthom.
I'm not gonna race him though.
I'm gonna put him out to stud."
- *Jack Woltz*

"She threw it all away
just to make me look ridiculous!
And a man in my position
can't afford to be made to look ridiculous!"
- Jack Woltz

"I need a man who has powerful friends.
I need a million dollars in cash.
I need, Don Corleone, those politicians that you
carry in your pockets
like so many nickels and dimes."

- Virgil Sollozzo

"I said that I would see you
because - I heard you were a serious man
- to be treated with respect."

- Don Vito Corleone

It's true - I have a lot of friends in politics - but they wouldn't be friendly very long if they knew my business was drugs instead of gambling, which they regard as a harmless vice - but drugs is a dirty business. It makes - it doesn't make any difference to me what a man does for a living, understand? But your business is - a little dangerous."

— Don Vito Corleone

"*I have a* sentimental weakness
for my children and I've spoiled them as
you can see. They talk when they should listen.
But – anyway - Signor Sollozzo, my *No* is final.
And I wish to congratulate you on
your new business; I know you'll do very well,
and – *good luck* ...
Especially since your interests
don't conflict with mine."
- *Don Vito Corleone*

"Never tell
anybody outside
the Family
what you're thinking again."

- Don Vito Corleone

"Leave the *gun*.

Take *the* cannolis."

– Pete Clemenza

"That's a Sicilian message.
It means Luca Brasi
sleeps with the fishes."

- Pete Clemenza

"That Sonny's runnin' wild.
He's thinking of goin'
to the mattresses already.
We gotta find a spot
over on the West Side."
- Pete Clemenza

"And watch out for the kids
when you're backin' out."
- Pete Clemenza

"Just lie here, Pop.
I'll take care of you now. I'm with you."
- *Michael Corleone*

"Put your hand in your pocket like you have a gun. You'll be alright."

- Michael Corleone

"Ah, I guess I'm getting too old for my job.
Too grouchy. Can't stand the aggravation.
You know how it is."

- Capt. McCluskey

"This is

BUSI

ﬧESS,

not personal."

— Tom Hagen

"What do you think this is,
the army, where you shoot 'em a mile away?
You gotta get up close,
like this – ba bing! You blow their brains
all over your nice Ivy League suit."

Sonny Corleone

Just let your hand drop to – your side
and let the gun slip out.
Everybody'll still think you got it.
They're gonna be starin at your face, Mike.
So walk outta the place real fast
but you don't run.
Don't look nobody in the eye
but you don't look away either.

- *Pete Clemenza*

"These things gotta happen
every five years or so – ten years –
helps get rid of the bad blood.
Been ten years since the last one.
You know you gotta stop 'em
at the beginning, like they shoulda
stopped Hitler at Munich."

- *Pete Clemenza*

"And don't take any chances.

Two shots in the head apiece."

- Pete Clemenza

"Listen, I want somebody good –
and I mean very good— to plant that gun.
I don't want my brother comin' out of that toilet
with just his dick in his hands, all right?"

- *Sonny Corleone*

"YOU GO TO THE RESTAURANT,

you eat, you talk for a while,
you relax. You make them relax.
Then you get up and you go take a leak.
No, better still -
you ask for permission to go."

- *Pete Clemenza*

"What guarantees can I give you, Mike?
I'm the hunted one!
I missed my chance.
You think too much of me, kid.
I'm not that clever."
- Virgil Sollozzo

"In Sicily women are more dangerous than shotguns."
- *Calo*

"Well Poppa never talked business at the table in front of the kids."
- Connie Brizzi

"Well , if I accepted that – in a court of law,
they could prove that I had knowledge
of his whereabouts."
- Tom Hagen

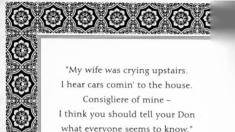

"My wife was crying upstairs.
I hear cars comin' to the house.
Consigliere of mine –
I think you should tell your Don
what everyone seems to know."

"I want – inquiries made.
I want no acts of vengeance.
I want you to arrange a meeting –
with the heads of the Five Families.
This war stops now."
- *Don Vito Corleone*

I want you to
use all your powers
and all your skills.
I don't want his mother
to see him this way.
Look, how they
massacred my boy."
- Don Vito Corleone

"I know English... Monday, Tuesday, Thursday, Wednesday, Friday, Sunday, Saturday..."

- *Appolonia Vitelli Corleone*

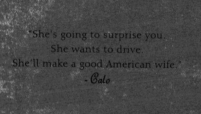

"She's going to surprise you.
She wants to drive.
She'll make a good American wife."

— *Calo*

"Look, we are all
reasonable men here;
we don't have to
give assurances as
if we were lawyers."
- Don Emilio Barzini

"You talk about vengeance. Is vengeance gonna
bring your son back to you? Or my boy to me?
I forego the vengeance of my son."

- *Don Vito Corleone*

"Tattalgia's a pimp.
He never could've out fought Santino.
But I didn't know it till this day that
it was – Barzini all along."
- Don Vito Corleone

"But I'm a superstitious man – and if
some unlucky accident should befall
him, if he should get shot in the head by
a police officer – or if he should hang himself in his jail cell – or if he is struck
by a bolt of lightning –
then I'm going to blame
some of the people in this room.
And that I do not forgive.
But – that aside – let me say that I swear –
on the souls of my grandchildren –
that I will not be the
one to break the peace that
we have made here today."

- Don Vito Corleone

"I thought you weren't going to become
a man like your father.
That's what you told me."
- *Kay Corleone*

"My father's no different
than any other powerful man."
- *Michael Corleone*

You know how naive you sound?
Senators and Presidents don't have men killed."

-Kay Corleone

"Do you have faith in my judgement?
Do I have your loyalty?

Then be a friend
to *Michael*
AND DO
as he says.'

- Don Vito Corleone

"*Yeah, well*

I'LL MAKE HIM AN OFFER

he *can't* refuse."

— *Michael Corleone*

"My credit good enough
to buy you out?"
- *Michael Corleone*

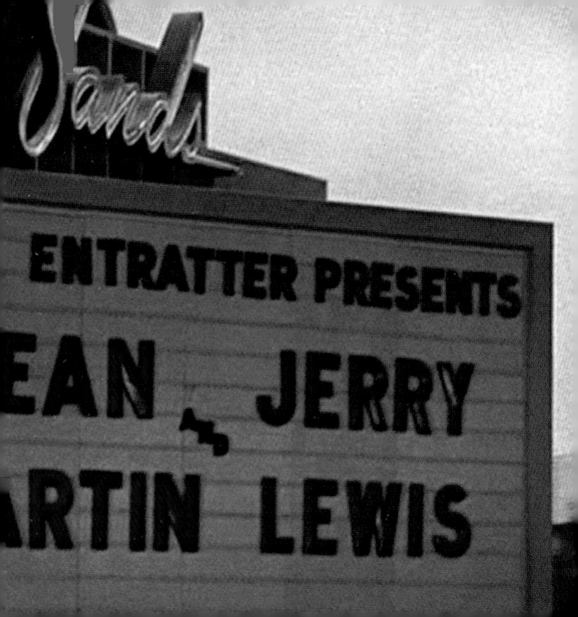
Sands
ENTRATTER PRESENTS
EAN JERRY
ARTIN LEWIS

"You don't come to Las Vegas and talk to
a man like Moe Green like that!

– Fredo Corleone

Fredo, you're my older brother, and I love you.
But don't take sides
with anyone against the Family again. Ever."
- *Michael Corleone*

"So, Barzini will move against you first. He'll set up a meeting with someone that you absolutely trust. Guaranteeing your safety. And at that meeting, you'll be assassinated."

- Don Vito Corleone

"I spend my life tryin' not to be careless.
Women and children
can be careless but not men."
- Don Vito Corleone

"But I never –
I never wanted this for you.
I work my whole life,
I don't apologize to take care of my family –
and I refused – to be a fool –
dancing on a string held by all those – big shots.
I don't apologize,
that's my life but I thought that
when it was your time, that

– that you would be the one to hold the strings.
Senator – Corleone –
Governor – Corleone, somethin'.
Well there just wasn't enough time, Michael;
just wasn't enough time."
- Don Vito Corleone

"Whoever comes to you with this Barzini meeting, he's the traitor. Don't forget that."
- Don Vito Corleone

"Tom, can you get me off the hook?
For old times sake?"
-Tessio

Priest: "Michael Francis Rizzi –

Do you renounce Satan?"

Michael: "I do renounce him."

"Come on,
do you think I'd make my sister a widow?
I'm godfather to your son, Carlo.
Go ahead, drink it, drink."
- Michael Corleone

"Only don't tell me you're innocent.
Because it insults my intelligence
– and makes me very angry.
Now, who approached you.
Tattaglia or Barzini?"
- *Michael Corleone*

1972
Mario Puzo's *The Godfather*
Runtime: 175 min
Directed by Francis Ford Coppola
Based on the novel
The Godfather by Mario Puzo
Screenplay by Mario Puzo and
Francis Ford Coppola

Cast overview, first billed only:
Marlon Brando .... Don Vito Corleone
Al Pacino .... Michael Corleone
James Caan .... Santino 'Sonny' Corleone
Richard S. Castellano .... Pete Clemenza
Robert Duvall .... Tom Hagen
Sterling Hayden .... Capt. Mark McCluskey
John Marley .... Jack Woltz
Richard Conte .... Emilio Barzini
Al Lettieri .... Virgil 'The Turk' Sollozzo
Diane Keaton .... Kay Adams
Abe Vigoda .... Salvatore "Sally" Tessio
Talia Shire .... Connie Corleone Rizzi
Gianni Russo .... Carlo Rizzi
John Cazale .... Fredo Corleone
Rudy Bond .... Carmine Cuneo
Al Martino .... Johnny Fontane
Morgana King .... Mama Corleone
Lenny Montana .... Luca Brasi
John Martino .... Paulie Gatto
Salvatore Corsitto .... Amerigo Bonasera
Richard Bright .... Al Neri
Alex Rocco .... Moe Greene
Tony Giorgio .... Bruno Tattaglia
Vito Scotti .... Nazorine

Tere Livrano .... Theresa Hagen
Victor Rendina .... Philip Tattaglia
Jeannie Linero .... Lucy Mancini
Julie Gregg .... Sandra Corleone
Ardell Sheridan .... Mrs. Clemenza
Simonetta Stefanelli ....
    Apollonia Vitelli-Corleone
Angelo Infanti .... Fabrizio
Corrado Gaipa .... Don Tommasino
Franco Citti .... Calo
Saro Urzì .... Vitelli
Rest of cast listed alphabetically:
Max Brandt .... Extra in
    furniture moving scene (uncredited)
Carmine Coppola .... Piano player
    in montage scene (uncredited)
Gian-Carlo Coppola ....
    Baptism observer (uncredited)
Sofia Coppola .... Michael Francis Rizzi
    (uncredited)
Ron Gilbert .... Usher in
    bridal party (uncredited)
Anthony Gounaris ....
    Anthony Vito Corleone (uncredited)
Joe Lo Grippo ....
    Sonny's bodyguard (uncredited)
Sonny Grosso .... Cop with Capt.
    McCluskey outside hospital (uncredited)
Louis Guss .... Don Zaluchi (outspoken
    Don at the Peace Conference) (uncredited)
Randy Jurgensen .... Sonny's Killer
    #1 (uncredited)
Tony Lip ....
    Wedding Guest (uncredited)

Frank Macetta .... (uncredited)
Lou Martini Jr. ....
   Boy at wedding (uncredited)
Father Joseph Medeglia ....
   Priest at baptism (uncredited)
Carol Morley .... Night Nurse (uncredited)
Rick Petrucelli .... Man in passenger seat
(when Michael is driven to the hospital)
(uncredited)
Burt Richards ....
   Floral designer (uncredited)
Sal Richards .... Drunk (uncredited)
Tom Rosqui ....
   Rocco Lampone (uncredited)
Nino Ruggeri .... mobster at funeral
   with Bazzini (uncredited)
Frank Sivero .... Extra (uncredited)
Filomena Spagnuolo .... Extra at wedding
   scene (uncredited)
Joe Spinell .... Willie Cicci (uncredited)
Gabriele Torrei .... Enzo Robutti
   (the baker) (uncredited)
Nick Vallelonga .... Wedding Party Guest
   (uncredited)
Ed Ventura .... Wedding guest (uncredited)
Matthew Vlahakis .... Clemenza's son
   (pushing toy car in driveway)
   (uncredited)

PRODUCED BY
Gray Frederickson .... associate producer
Albert S. Ruddy .... producer

ORIGINAL MUSIC BY
Nino Rota
Cinematography by
Gordon Willis
Film Editing by
William Reynolds
Peter Zinner

CASTING BY
Louis DiGiaimo (as Louis Digiaimo)
Andrea Eastman
Fred Roos

PRODUCTION DESIGN BY
Dean Tavoularis

ART DIRECTION BY
Warren Clymer

SET DECORATION BY
Philip Smith

COSTUME DESIGN BY
Anna Hill Johnstone

MAKEUP DEPARTMENT
Philip Leto .... hair stylist (as Phil Leto)
Phil Rhodes .... makeup artist (as Philip
Rhodes)
Dick Smith .... makeup artist

PRODUCTION MANAGEMENT

Fred C. Caruso .... unit production
    manager (as Fred Caruso)
Valerio De Paolis .... production manager:
    Sicily (as Valerio DePaolis)
Ned Kopp .... production manager:
    second unit (uncredited)

Second Unit Director or Assistant Director
Tony Brandt .... assistant director: Sicily
Fred T. Gallo .... assistant director
    (as Fred Gallo)
Steven P. Skloot .... second
    assistant director

ART DEPARTMENT

Samuel Verts .... assistant
    art director: Sicily

SOUND DEPARTMENT

Howard Beals .... sound effects editor
Charles Grenzbach .... sound re-recordist
    (as Bud Grenzbach)
Christopher Newman .... production
    sound recordist
Richard Portman .... sound re-recordist
John C. Hammell .... music editor
    (uncredited)
Pierre Jalbert .... assistant sound
    editor (uncredited)

SPECIAL EFFECTS BY

Sass Bedig .... special effects
A.D. Flowers .... special effects
Joe Lombardi .... special effects
Paul J. Lombardi .... special effects
    supervisor (uncredited)

STUNTS

Paul Baxley .... stunt coordinator
    (uncredited)
Joe Bucaro III .... stunt double: young
    Vincenzo (uncredited)
Steven Burnett .... stunts (uncredited)

OTHER CREW

Robert Barth .... unit coordinator
Tony Bowers .... location coordinator
Michael Briggs .... location coordinator
Michael Chapman .... camera operator
Gary Chazan .... assistant to producer
Nancy Hopton .... continuity
    (as Nancy Tonery)
Robert S. Mendelsohn .... executive
    assistant to producer
Walter Murch .... post-production
    consultant
George Newman .... wardrobe supervisor
Marilyn Putnam .... wardrobe: women
Carlo Savina .... conductor
Peter Zinner .... foreign post-production

13 Digit ISBN: 978-1-60433-233-9
10 Digit ISBN: 1-60433-233-6

This book may be ordered by mail from the publisher.
Please include $2.75 for postage and handling.
Please support your local bookseller first!

Books published by Cider Mill Press Book Publishers are available at special discounts for bulk purchases in the United States by corporations, institutions, and other organizations. For more information, please contact the publisher.

Cider Mill Press Book Publishers
"Where good books are ready for press"
12 Port Farm Road
Kennebunkport, Maine 04046

Visit us on the web!
www.cidermillpress.com

Design by Bashan Aquart, Dan Kenneally
Printed in China

1 2 3 4 5 6 7 8 9 0
First Edition

ABOUT THE AUTHOR

Carlo De Vito is a long time publishing executive and is also the editor of *The International Encyclopedia of World Organized Crime*. He lives in Freehold, New Jersey and Hudson, New York, with his wife, sons Dylan and Dawson, and their dogs.

ABOUT CIDER MILL PRESS BOOK PUBLISHERS

Good ideas ripen with time. From seed to harvest, Cider Mill Press strives to bring fine reading, information, and entertainment together between the covers of its creatively crafted books. Our Cider Mill bears fruit twice a year, publishing a new crop of titles each Spring and Fall.

Visit us on the web at
www.cidermillpress.com
or write to us at
12 Port Farm Road
Kennebunkport, Maine 04046